M000110664

Cling Journal

Drawing Closer to God Through the Book of James

Kim Cash Tate

Copyright © 2018 by Kim Cash Tate.

All rights reserved. No part of this publication may be reproduced, distributed, or transmitted in any form or by any means, including photocopying, recording, or other electronic or mechanical methods, without prior written permission of the author, except in the case of brief quotations embedded in critical views and certain other noncommercial uses permitted by copyright law.
Scripture quotations are taken from the New American Standard Bible ®, Copyright © 1960, 1962, 1963, 1968, 1971, 1972, 1973, 1975, 1977, 1995 by The Lockman Foundation. Used by permission.

Cover design and interior layout: Spechouse Creative
Tate, Kimberly Cash.
Cling Journal – Drawing Closer to God Through the Book of James / Kim Cash Tate.
ISBN: 978-1-946336-03-3

ALSO BY KIM CASH TATE

Heavenly Places
Faithful
Cherished
Hope Springs
The Color of Hope
Hidden Blessings
Though I Stumble
If I Believe
If You're With Me
When I'm Tempted

Cling: Choosing a Lifestyle of Intimacy with God

Introduction

"How do you cling to God?"

I get that question often, and my answer is rather simple. I talk to Him—a lot. I get to know Him through His word. And often, I'm talking to Him *about* His word. More than anything, that's what has caused my walk with God to grow deeper. As I study His word, I talk to Him about the ways in which it is challenging me, convicting me, strengthening me, and uplifting me. I ask for help in understanding and applying His word. I praise Him as I read His word, often pausing at a verse that blows me away, and telling Him, "Lord, You are so amazing."

That's the heart behind this journal—to guide you into a closer walk with God, as you walk through the book of James. You won't find questions that lead you to simply reflect and write a response. You will find prompts that are direct responses to particular verses. And every prompt is meant to take you to the Lord, through prayer, thanksgiving, and praise. The idea is to write your responses directly to God, as a prayer.

Keep in mind, though—these prompts are my own. I'm calling them, "Ways to Cling," hoping that they will be a useful guide. But please don't feel that you have to follow every prompt. Adopt what you find helpful. Substitute your own. The key is to take your thoughts, questions, praises, convictions, and burdens with respect to the given verses—directly to the Lord. Keep in mind as well that this journal does not include every verse from the book of James. Thus, at the end of each section, there is space for you to seek the Lord about additional verses from that particular chapter.

Introduction

Finally, you can find the Cling Bible study on the book of James on my YouTube channel (YouTube.com/kimcashtate). But you don't need to watch that study in order to move through the journal. The only indispensable tool you need is your Bible.

This journal is between you and God. I pray that you draw near to Him in these pages. And because His word is true—and God is faithful—I'm praising Him already that He will also draw near to You.

Blessings to you as you cling to Him!

Kim Cash Tate

*"James, a bond-servant of God
and of the Lord Jesus Christ . . ." (James 1:1)*

Ways To Cling

As a believer, give God praise that you are no longer a slave of sin and of the enemy because you've been redeemed by the precious blood of Jesus.

Thank Jesus for His sacrificial death on the cross on your behalf. Ask the Lord to give you the heart of a bond-servant, as one whose will is consumed in the will of Jesus.

Ask the Lord to ground you in your identity as a bond-servant of God and of the Lord Jesus Christ.

Confess that you are not always willing to exchange your will for the Lord's will.

Ask for grace and strength to submit your will to the will of God.

Drawing Closer To God  Through The Book Of James

"Consider it all joy, my brethren, when you encounter various trials, knowing that the testing of your faith produces endurance. And let endurance have its perfect result, so that you may be perfect and complete, lacking in nothing."
(James 1:2-4)

Ways To Cling

Think about the trials you are currently facing. Be real with God about your fears, doubts, worries, disappointments, and heartaches.

Ask God to help you to cling to Him through this current hardship.

Ask Him to help you to consider it all joy, knowing that this trial is producing endurance. Thank Him that His joy is your strength (Nehemiah 8:10).

Think about a former trial in which God showed His faithfulness. Thank Him even now that He is a faithful God.

Ask God to show you what you need to do to let endurance have its perfect result. Ask for grace and strength to do so.

By faith thank God for all the ways in which this trial is making you perfect and complete in Christ.

Praise God that "He who began a work in you will perfect it until the day of Christ Jesus" (Philippians 1:6).

Drawing Closer To God **cling** *JOURNAL* Through The Book Of James

Drawing Closer To God **cling** JOURNAL *Through The Book Of James*

"But if any of you lacks wisdom, let him ask of God, who gives to all generously and without reproach, and it will be given to him. But he must ask in faith without any doubting . . ." (James 1:5-6)

Ways To Cling

Confess to God that it's hard to "consider it all joy" and to "let endurance have its perfect result."

Ask the Lord for wisdom. Humbly acknowledge that you can't endure without Him.

Ask the Lord for ears to hear the wisdom He provides and for grace to walk it out.

Confess any doubts that you may have as to God's ability or willingness to help.

Ask the Lord to help your unbelief and to increase your faith. Praise Him and thank Him for the promise that wisdom will be given.

Thank Him for His goodness in giving wisdom generously and without reproach.

Drawing Closer To God **cling** *Through The Book Of James*
JOURNAL

"But the brother of humble circumstances is to glory in his high position; and the rich man is to glory in his humiliation, because like flowering grass he will fade away." (James 1:9-10)

Ways To Cling

Ask the Lord to give you an eternal perspective with respect to your current economic situation.

Give God praise for your "high position"—that you have been raised up with Christ and seated with Him in heavenly places (Ephesians 2:6).

Ask the Lord to deepen your understanding of your position in Christ and how to walk in light of it.

Ask the Lord to show you whether you glory in earthly possessions. Ask Him to give you His view of those possessions.

Ask God to help you to glory in the humble truth that you will one day fade away from this earth.

_____
_____
_____
_____
_____
_____
_____
_____
_____
_____
_____
_____
_____
_____
_____
_____
_____
_____
_____
_____
_____
_____
_____
_____
_____
_____
_____

"But each one is tempted when he is carried away and enticed by his own lust. Then when lust has conceived, it gives birth to sin; and when sin is accomplished, it brings forth death."
(James 1:14-15)

Ways To Cling

Ask God to show you your lusts. Ask Him to reveal the hidden longings of your heart.

Ask God to protect you from being tempted in those areas. Pray to be able to spot those temptations at the outset and for strength such that you don't enter into them.

Ask for wisdom to avoid situations in which you might be tempted.

Be real with God about areas in which you are being tempted right now. Tell Him where you are weak and vulnerable.

Ask the Lord to show you where you are weak and vulnerable, since you may not be fully aware.

If you are being carried away and enticed by your lust, be real with God about that. Tell Him how you are feeling. Confess that your flesh longs to indulge the temptation. Ask for His power to strengthen you to flee the temptation.

If you are in sin, ask the Lord for eyes to view that sin as He views it. Ask Him for a heart that grieves that sin.

"But each one is tempted when he is carried away and enticed by his own lust. Then when lust has conceived, it gives birth to sin; and when sin is accomplished, it brings forth death."
(James 1:14-15)

Ways To Cling

(Continued)

With a sincere heart, confess your sin to God.

Ask for the Lord's power to deliver you from sin. Praise Him that He is able to deliver.

Ask God to put someone in your path who can help you and walk with you through this.

If you are feeling far from God as a result of sin, be real with God about that. Tell Him how you feel. Ask Him for help to draw near. Thank Him that His word is true, that He wants you to cling to Him.

Drawing Closer To God Through The Book Of James

JOURNAL

Drawing Closer To God Through The Book Of James

"Every good thing given and every perfect gift is from above, coming down from the Father of lights, with whom there is no variation or shifting shadow." (James 1:17)

Ways To Cling

Give God praise that He is the giver of good things and perfect gifts.

Thank God for specific things He has given you, including spiritual blessings like joy and peace.

Ask God to show you good things He has given and perfect gifts that you haven't recognized as coming from Him.

Give Him praise because "God is Light, and in Him there is no darkness at all" (1 John 1:5).

Ask the Father of lights to shine light on the dark places in your life.

Drawing Closer To God **cling** JOURNAL Through The Book Of James

"This you know, my beloved brethren. But everyone must be quick to hear, slow to speak and slow to anger . . ."
(James 1:19)

Ways To Cling

Confess that your posture is more often the opposite — slow to hear and quick to speak.

Ask God to cultivate in you a listening heart.

Ask the Lord to help you to guard your tongue.

Pray for a heart of humility to receive the truth of the word of God.

Pray for a temperament that is peaceful and not easily provoked.

Drawing Closer To God  Through The Book Of James

"But prove yourselves doers of the word, and not merely hearers who delude themselves." (James 1:22)

Ways To Cling

Consider those areas in which you know that you are not abiding by the word of God. Confess it to God as sin.

Ask the Lord to help you to grow in obeying His word.

Ask Him to show you where you have already grown in obeying His word. Praise Him for His grace at work in your life.

Ask the Lord to show you what changes you need to make to walk in obedience in a specific area. Thank Him in advance for giving you the grace to do so.

Ask God to show you whether you are merely a hearer who is deluding yourself.

"Pure and undefiled religion in the sight of our God and Father is this: to visit orphans and widows in their distress, and to keep oneself unstained by the world." (James 1:27)

Ways To Cling

Ask the Lord to give you a heart for orphans, widows, and others who are often overlooked.

Ask Him to show you someone to whom you can be a blessing, by visiting or helping in some way.

Praise God that He has a heart for those in need, such as orphans and widows.

Ask the Lord to show you where you may be "stained" by the world.

Ask the Lord what you need to do specifically to keep yourself unstained by the world.

Drawing Closer To God · cling JOURNAL · Through The Book Of James

Drawing Closer To God **cling** JOURNAL Through The Book Of James

Additional Thoughts

Drawing Closer To God **cling** Through The Book Of James
JOURNAL

"My brethren, do not hold your faith in our glorious Lord Jesus Christ with an attitude of personal favoritism." (James 2:1)

Ways To Cling

Ask the Lord to examine your heart and reveal where you show favoritism toward one type of person over another.

Confess what God reveals as sin.

Ask the Lord to give you His heart toward those people that you don't naturally favor.

Ask Him to give you eyes to see the people that you tend to overlook.

Give God praise because He is a God who "sees not as man sees, for man looks at the outward appearance, but the LORD looks at the heart" (1 Samuel 16:9).

Ask the Lord to give you eyes to see as He sees.

Drawing Closer To God **cling** JOURNAL Through The Book Of James

Drawing Closer To God   **cling** *JOURNAL*   Through The Book Of James

*"If, however, you are fulfilling the royal law according to the
Scripture, 'YOU SHALL LOVE YOUR NEIGHBOR AS YOURSELF,'
you are doing well." (James 2:8)*

Ways To Cling

Thank the Lord that His love "has been poured out within our
hearts through the Holy Spirit who was given to us" (Romans
5:5).

Ask God to help you to walk in love in tangible ways with
others.

Ask God to show you someone specific for whom you do not
have love. Confess what God reveals as sin. Ask God to give
you His heart for this person.

Praise God that He loved you first, before you loved Him (1
John 4:19).

Drawing Closer To God  Through The Book Of James

"For judgment will be merciless to one who has shown no mercy;
mercy triumphs over judgment." (James 2:13)

Ways To Cling

Consider the judgment you deserve for sin ("For the wages
of sin is death, but the free gift of God is eternal life in
Christ Jesus our Lord" (Romans 6:23)). Praise God that He
was rich in mercy in saving you.

Ask the Lord to show you whether you are merciful toward
others.

If your heart is pricked as to an instance in which you did
not show mercy, ask the Lord to forgive you. Seek the Lord
as to how you can make that right.

Ask God to give you a heart of mercy.

Give God praise for the truth that mercy triumphs over judgment.

If you have the gift of mercy, ask the Lord for grace to stew-
ard that gift well. Ask Him to show you ways to use your gift
for the benefit of others.

"Even so faith, if it has no works, is dead, being by itself."
(James 2:17)

Ways To Cling

Give God praise for the gift of salvation—"For by grace you have been saved through faith; and that not of yourselves, it is the gift of God; not as a result of works, so that no one may boast" (Ephesians 2:8-9).

Be real with God about any doubts you may have as to whether your faith is dead or alive.

Ask the Lord whether your faith is alive, that is, whether you have been made "alive together with Christ" (Ephesians 2:5) through salvation by grace through faith.

Ask God to give you a living faith, that is, salvation through His Son, Jesus Christ.

Give God thanks and praise for the works you've seen in your life as a result of faith in Jesus.

Ephesians 2:10 says, "For we are His workmanship, created in Christ Jesus for good works, which God prepared beforehand so that we would walk in them." Ask the Lord to continually reveal the good works He prepared beforehand for you in Christ (Ephesians 2:10), and for grace to walk in them.

Through The Book Of James

Drawing Closer To God   Through The Book Of James

JOURNAL

Drawing Closer To God  Through The Book Of James

Additional Thoughts

"Let not many of you become teachers, my brethren, knowing that as such we will incur a stricter judgment." (James 3:1)

Ways To Cling

If you feel called to teach the word of God in any capacity, ask the Lord to confirm that calling.

Ask God to give you a love of His word and an ever-increasing hunger to prayerfully study His word.

Ask the Lord to give you grace to "Be diligent to present yourself approved to God as a workman who does not need to be ashamed, accurately handling the word of truth." (2 Timothy 2:15)

Pray for a spirit of humility as you study and teach His word. Confess as sin those times you have taught the word of God in a careless manner.

Give God thanks and praise for the Holy Spirit who teaches us and helps us understand truth in the word.

Pray to not only teach the word well but to walk in obedience to it.

Drawing Closer To God **cling** JOURNAL Through The Book Of James

"But no one can tame the tongue; it is a restless evil and full of deadly poison." (James 3:8)

Ways To Cling

Consider the ways in which you have stumbled with your tongue lately. Ask God for forgiveness.

Ask God to tame your tongue.

Give God praise that nothing is too hard for Him, not even taming the tongue.

Pray that the words of your mouth and the meditation of your heart be acceptable in God's sight (Psalm 19:14).

Pray that your words bring healing; pray that your words be good for edification according to the need of the moment, giving grace to those who hear (Ephesians 4:29).

Ask God how you can use your tongue today for His glory.

Drawing Closer To God · cling JOURNAL · Through The Book Of James

Drawing Closer To God **cling** Through The Book Of James

JOURNAL

"With it we bless our Lord and Father, and with it we curse men, who have been made in the likeness of God . . ." (James 3:9)

Ways To Cling

Ask God to forgive you for serving two masters with your tongue—the Lord and your flesh.

Ask God to show you whether there is someone you need to go to and ask forgiveness for your words.

Ask the Lord for eyes to see others, even those we may not naturally like, as made in His likeness.

Give God praise that you have been made in His image. Ask Him for eyes to see yourself as fearfully and wonderfully made (Psalm 139:14).

Ask the Lord to give you grace to bless others with your words. Ask specifically for one person whom you can bless in this way today.

Think about ways in which others have blessed you with their words lately. Give thanks to God for moving in their hearts to do so.

"But if you have bitter jealousy and selfish ambition in your heart, do not be arrogant and so lie against the truth. This wisdom is not that which comes down from above, but is earthly, natural, demonic." (James 3:14-15)

Ways To Cling

Ask God to reveal whether the wisdom you exhibit is from above or of this world.

Ask God to reveal whether you have bitter jealousy and/or selfish ambition in your heart. If so, confess it as sin. Ask the Lord to exchange earthly wisdom for His wisdom.

Given that "Satan disguises himself as an angel of light" (2 Corinthians 11:14), his wisdom often appears as light as well. Pray for discernment that you may know and walk in the wisdom that is from above.

Ask the Lord to convict you when you lean on your own understanding as a form of "natural" wisdom.

Give thanks to God that He so liberally gives wisdom from above.

Give God praise for His goodness in letting us know the fruit of earthly wisdom verses the fruit of godly wisdom.

"But the wisdom from above is first pure, then peaceable, gentle, reasonable, full of mercy and good fruits, unwavering, without hypocrisy." (James 3:17)

Ways To Cling

Give God praise for the good and perfect attributes of His wisdom.

Pray to walk in wisdom that is pure, including purity of thought and purity of devotion to God.

Ask the Lord for a peaceable and gentle spirit.

Ask the Lord to help you to be reasonable in your dealings with others.

Pray for a heart that is full of mercy and good fruits.
Pray to be unwavering in your commitment to truth and your devotion to Jesus.

Pray for a Christian walk that is without hypocrisy.

Give thanks to God for the ways in which you have already grown in godly wisdom.

Drawing Closer To God **cling** *JOURNAL* Through The Book Of James

_____

_____

_____

_____

_____

_____

_____

_____

_____

_____

_____

_____

_____

_____

_____

_____

_____

_____

_____

_____

_____

_____

_____

_____

_____

_____

_____

_____

_____

Drawing Closer To God **cling** Through The Book Of James

JOURNAL

Drawing Closer To God   **cling** JOURNAL   Through The Book Of James

Additional Thoughts

Drawing Closer To God   **cling**   Through The Book Of James
JOURNAL

"You ask and do not receive, because you ask with wrong motives, so that you may spend it on your pleasures."
(James 4:3)

Ways To Cling

Ask the Lord to search your heart as to your motives in the things you ask of Him.

Ask forgiveness for praying with selfish motives.

Give thanks to God for not answering prayers that you prayed with wrong motives.

Ask God to give you a heart that longs to glorify Him.
Ask the Lord to exchange your will for His will. Pray, "Your will be done, Lord."

Jesus said, "If you abide in Me, and My words abide in you, ask whatever you wish, and it will be done for you" (John 15:7). Ask the Lord to show you how to abide in Him, and how to have His words abide in you.

Ask the Lord to give you a godly confidence to pray for those things that are in accordance with His will.

Drawing Closer To God

JOURNAL

Through The Book Of James

Drawing Closer To God **cling** JOURNAL Through The Book Of James

"You adulteresses, do you not know that friendship with the world is hostility toward God? Therefore whoever wishes to be a friend of the world makes himself an enemy of God."
(James 4:4)

Ways To Cling

Ask the Lord to show you whether you are a friend of the world.

Ask the Lord whether there is anything about the world that you embrace which is contrary to His word and His ways.

If the Lord convicts your heart in response to the questions above, ask forgiveness with a sincere heart. Thank Him that He is faithful and righteous to forgive us our sins and to cleanse us from all unrighteousness.

Give God praise that the god of this world will be thrown into the lake of fire and will be "tormented day and night forever and ever" (Revelation 20:10).

Give God praise that he who believes that Jesus is the Son of God overcomes the world (1 John 5:5).

Ask the Lord to help you to love people in the world without embracing the ways of the world.

Drawing Closer To God **cling** Through The Book Of James
JOURNAL

Drawing Closer To God *cling* Through The Book Of James

"Submit therefore to God. Resist the devil and he will flee from you." (James 4:7)

Ways To Cling

Ask the Lord for a heart of submission.

Decide before the Lord that you will submit to Him. Thank Him for the grace to do so.

Ask the Lord to show you what a life of submission unto Him looks like.

Pray for strength to resist the devil and for protection from his schemes.

Pray for discernment to know when you are dealing with the schemes of the enemy.

Give God praise that when we submit to Him and resist the devil, the devil will flee.

Praise God that "greater is He who is in you than he who is in the world" (1 John 4:4).

Drawing Closer To God cling JOURNAL Through The Book Of James

Drawing Closer To God **cling** JOURNAL Through The Book Of James

"Draw near to God, and He will draw near to you. Cleanse your hands, you sinners; and purify your hearts, you double-minded. Be miserable and mourn and weep; let your laughter be turned into mourning and your joy to gloom."
(James 4:8-9)

Ways To Cling

Set aside a special time and place to draw near to God. Sit in His presence.

Spend prayerful time in the word of God. Ask the Lord to speak to your heart.

Give God praise that He will draw near to you when you draw near to Him.

Ask the Lord if there is unconfessed sin in your life. Pray for a heart that mourns and weeps over your sin. Thank Him that He is faithful and righteous to forgive your sin, and to cleanse you from all unrighteousness (1 John 1:9).

Ask the Lord to purify your heart. Like David, pray, "Create in me a clean heart, O God, and renew a steadfast spirit within me" (Psalm 51:10).

Ask the Lord to show you how you can draw near and delight yourself in Him daily.

Drawing Closer To God **cling** JOURNAL Through The Book Of James

Drawing Closer To God **cling** *JOURNAL* Through The Book Of James

"Humble yourselves in the presence of the Lord, and He will exalt you." (James 4:10)

Ways To Cling

Ask the Lord for a heart of humility before Him.

Praise the Lord that He is the vine, and you are the branch; if you abide in Him, you bear much fruit, but apart from Him you can do nothing (John 15:5).

Give God praise that He will exalt you in His time, in accordance with His will.

Ask the Lord for grace to wait on Him, and to resist the temptation to exalt yourself.

Spend regular time in the presence of the Lord. Tell the Lord you need Him every moment. Thank Him that He is there every moment.

"Yet you do not know what your life will be like tomorrow. You are just a vapor that appears for a little while and then vanishes away." (James 4:14)

Ways To Cling

Confess that you have been given to planning for the future without acknowledging the Lord.

Give God praise that your times are in His hand (Psalm 31:15) and that all your days were ordained "when as yet there was not one of them" (Psalm 139:16).

Ask the Lord to show you His plans for you, and to establish them in your life.

Ask Him to redirect you in any plans you have made outside of His will.

Ask the Lord how you can glorify Him in the short time you have on earth.

Thank the Lord that your life, with its trials and tribulations, is short here on earth, while eternity with Him is forever.

"Therefore, to one who knows the right thing to do and does not do it, to him it is sin." (James 4:17)

Ways To Cling

Ask the Lord to reveal the right things you know to do—which you are not doing.

Confess as sin whatever you are doing or not doing that is contrary to the will of God.

Ask for strength and grace to walk in obedience to God's will.

Ask the Lord to burden your heart when you move outside of His will, such that you will be moved to repent.

Give God praise that He is a gracious God who freely forgives.

Drawing Closer To God  Through The Book Of James

Drawing Closer To God **cling** JOURNAL Through The Book Of James

Drawing Closer To God · Through The Book Of James

Additional Thoughts

Drawing Closer To God **cling** JOURNAL Through The Book Of James

"Therefore be patient, brethren, until the coming of the Lord. The farmer waits for the precious produce of the soil, being patient about it, until it gets the early and late rains. You too be patient; strengthen your hearts, for the coming of the Lord is near." (James 5:7-8)

Ways To Cling

Praise the Lord that He is coming soon. Ask the Lord how to live in the light of this truth.

Ask for patience as you endure various trials, knowing that your current situation will not last always.

Give God praise that "momentary, light affliction is producing for us an eternal weight of glory far beyond all comparison" (2 Corinthians 4:17).

Ask God to strengthen your heart continually.

Give God praise that He is able to command your strength (Psalm 68:28).

Ask the Lord to help you to fix your eyes on Jesus, the author and perfecter of faith (Hebrews 12:2).

Ask the Lord to help you to "look not at the things which are seen, but at the things which are not seen; for the things which are seen are temporal, but the things which are not seen are eternal" (2 Corinthians 4:18).

"Do not complain, brethren, against one another, so that you yourselves may not be judged; behold, the Judge is standing right at the door." (James 5:9)

Ways To Cling

Consider whether you have grumbled and complained against someone of late. Confess it as sin.

Pray for grace to be able to overlook offenses. Pray to be quick to forgive.

Ask the Lord for grace to "do all things without grumbling or disputing; so that you will prove yourselves to be blameless and innocent, children of God above reproach in the midst of a crooked and perverse generation, among whom you appear as lights in the world" (Philippians 2:14-15).

Give God praise that He is a righteous Judge.

Drawing Closer To God   cling   Through The Book Of James
JOURNAL

Drawing Closer To God **cling** JOURNAL Through The Book Of James

"We count those blessed who endured. You have heard of the endurance of Job and have seen the outcome of the Lord's dealings, that the Lord is full of compassion and is merciful." (James 5:11)

Ways To Cling

Give God praise for His grace upon Job to endure. Thank Him that He is not a respecter of persons. If He gave Job grace to endure, He will supply the grace you need as well.

Praise God that He is full of compassion and merciful.

Give thanks to God for the compassion and mercy He has shown you.

Give thanks to God for giving us examples in His word of those who have endured through the ages, as encouragement for us. Praise God because He is faithful.

If you are in the midst of a trial, pray that the Lord would show compassion and mercy.

Drawing Closer To God **cling** JOURNAL Through The Book Of James

"But above all, my brethren, do not swear, either by heaven or by earth or with any other oath; but your yes is to be yes, and your no, no, so that you may not fall under judgment." (James 5:12)

Ways To Cling

Ask the Lord to show you whether you use "oaths" in your speech to emphasize that you are being honest. If so, ask for help to eliminate those.

Ask for grace in your dealings with others such that your yes will be yes, and your no, no.

Pray for courage to say no without making up excuses.

Ask the Lord to help you to lay aside falsehood (even omissions) and speak truth (Ephesians 4:25).

Drawing Closer To God cling JOURNAL Through The Book Of James

"Is anyone among you suffering? Then he must pray. Is anyone cheerful? He is to sing praises." (James 5:13)

Ways To Cling

If you are suffering through a trial, lay your cares before the Lord. Ask for patience and strength to endure. Ask for wisdom. Cultivate a lifestyle of prayer by talking to God throughout the day.

Give thanks to God that He will never leave you nor forsake you (Hebrews 13:5).

Give thanks to God that He "causes all things to work together for good to those who love God, to those who are called according to His purpose" (Romans 8:28).

Ask God to work this current situation for good. Pray that He be glorified in it.

Praise God that His joy is your strength (Nehemiah 8:10). Put on your favorite praise music. Sing praises unto God. Lift your heart in worship.

Drawing Closer To God — cling JOURNAL — Through The Book Of James

*"Therefore, confess your sins to one another, and pray for
one another so that you may be healed. The effective
prayer of a righteous man can accomplish much."*
(James 5:16)

Ways To Cling

Ask the Lord to show you someone trustworthy to whom you
can confess your sins.

Ask for courage to be vulnerable and humble as you confess
how you have fallen short.

Pray to be a person who is trustworthy, to whom others can
confess their sins.

Pray to have a listening and loving heart when someone con-
fesses her sin to you.

Pray for those whom the Lord has entrusted into your care.
Thank the Lord for using you in the lives of others as an
instrument of healing.

Give God praise for the power of prayer. Thank Him for using
prayer in such mighty ways.

Ask the Lord to increase your confidence in the power of
prayer. Pray that you would not hesitate to go boldly before
the throne of our God.

Drawing Closer To God **cling** JOURNAL Through The Book Of James

Drawing Closer To God  Through The Book Of James

"My brethren, if any among you strays from the truth and one turns him back, let him know that he who turns a sinner from the error of his way will save his soul from death and will cover a multitude of sins." *(James 5:19-20)*

Ways To Cling

Ask the Lord for eyes to see when He has put someone in your path, in order for you to help turn them toward the truth.

Ask the Lord for a loving and patient heart in dealing with others who are in sin. Pray as well that you do not compromise the truth.

Ask the Lord for wisdom to know what to say and do as you walk alongside this individual.

Give God praise that He desires to save souls from death and cover a multitude of sins.

Give God praise for saving your own soul from death and covering your sins.

Thank the Lord for the ministry of His Spirit, and the grace to do what He calls us to do, for His glory.

Drawing Closer To God  Through The Book Of James

Drawing Closer To God **cling** JOURNAL Through The Book Of James

Drawing Closer To God **cling** JOURNAL Through The Book Of James

Drawing Closer To God Through The Book Of James

Additional Thoughts

Drawing Closer To God **cling** JOURNAL Through The Book Of James

Made in the USA
Las Vegas, NV
07 November 2021

33904875R00120